AMERICA

AMERICAN HEART ASSOCIATION
COOKBOOK, 5TH EDITION

AMERICAN HEART ASSOCIATION
LOW-FAT, LOW-CHOLESTEROL
COOKBOOK

AMERICAN HEART ASSOCIATION
LOW-SALT COOKBOOK

AMERICAN HEART ASSOCIATION
FAT AND CHOLESTEROL COUNTER

AMERICAN HEART ASSOCIATION

FAT

AND

CHOLESTEROL

C·O·U·N·T·E·R

BY THE
AMERICAN HEART ASSOCIATION

TIMES BOOKS

RANDOM HOUSE

LIBRARY OF CONGRESS CATALOGING-IN-PUBLICATION DATA

American Heart Association fat and cholesterol counter / by American Heart Association.

    p.   cm.

  ISBN 0-8129-1885-1

  1. Food—Cholesterol content—Tables.

2. Food—Fat content—Tables. 3. Food—Sodium content—Tables. I. American Heart Association. II. Title: Fat and cholesterol counter.

TX553.C43A44 1991

641.1′4—dc20   90-50216

Designed by Beth Tondreau Design

Manufactured in the United States of America

9 8 7 6 5 4 3 2

CONTENTS

AMERICAN HEART ASSOCIATION
FAT AND CHOLESTEROL COUNTER

INTRODUCTION

Eating Your Heart Out

THE evidence is in. We can't ignore it.

Hundreds of scientific studies show a strong link between a diet high in saturated fat and cholesterol and the development of atherosclerosis. We know that atherosclerosis is one of the major causes of heart attack and stroke.

Atherosclerosis is a progressive disease of the blood vessels. Fatty substances, mostly cholesterol, build up in the inner lining of the arteries. This can eventually block an artery and stop the flow of blood. When this happens in an artery that supplies blood to your heart, you have a heart attack. When it happens in an artery feeding your brain, you have a stroke.

Cholesterol is a major part of the fatty build-up known as atherosclerotic plaque. It comes mostly from your bloodstream. And the cholesterol in your blood comes from two places: your body produces a great deal of it, and you get some of it from the foods you eat. People with a high level of cholesterol in their blood are at much higher risk of having a heart attack than those who keep their cholesterol levels low.

Down with High Cholesterol

MOST heart attacks that happen in middle age and later life are caused by long-standing high blood cholesterol, most often caused by a diet high in total fat, saturated fat and cholesterol.

Studies show that the higher your blood cholesterol rises above 200 mg/dl, the more likely it is that you will have a heart attack.

The National Cholesterol Education Program is a program of the National Heart, Lung, and Blood Institute (NHLBI). It has established the following guidelines for determining how blood cholesterol levels relate to the risk of heart disease.

While it's important to keep your blood cholesterol level below 200 mg/dl, your body does need some blood cholesterol. It helps produce sex hormones and form cell membranes and protective sheaths around your nerves. Fortunately, your body manufactures the amount of cholesterol you need for this. You don't really need any of the cholesterol that comes from food.

CLASSIFICATION BASED ON TOTAL CHOLESTEROL

CHOLESTEROL LEVEL	RISK
Less than 200 mg/dl	Desirable
200–239 mg/dl	Borderline high
240 mg/dl or greater	High

Cholesterol Isn't Your Only Worry

BESIDES high blood cholesterol, several other major factors can increase your risk for heart disease. These include cigarette smoking, high blood pressure, excess body weight and diabetes.

To help control your risk factors for heart attack and stroke, it's important to cut down on the saturated fat and cholesterol in your diet. It's also important to limit your sodium intake, quit smoking, control your blood pressure, exercise, and keep your weight at its optimum level.

A Diet You Can
Put Your Heart Into

THE American Heart Association Diet is a simple eating plan for all healthy Americans over the age of two.

It offers these few easy-to-follow guidelines that can help you control your blood cholesterol level by controlling the amount and kind of fat you eat and limiting your dietary cholesterol. If you follow the basic plan, your body will get all of the essential nutrients it needs.

And, when you compare the diet recommendations from the American Heart Association, the American Cancer Society, the American Diabetes Association and the United States Department of Agriculture/Health and Human Services (USDA/HHS) Dietary Guidelines, you'll find that they share the same basic concept. So when you follow the American Heart Association guidelines outlined below, you're not only taking steps to prevent heart disease, you may also help prevent some forms of cancer and control diabetes.

AMERICAN HEART ASSOCIATION DIET GUIDELINES

- Limit your intake of meat, seafood and poultry to no more than 6 ounces per day.
- Eat only lean meats, fish and poultry.
- Trim or drain away all fat from meats, fish and poultry.
- Use meatless main dishes as entrees, or cook "low-meat" entrees by combining small amounts of meat with rice, pasta, beans or vegetables.
- Use approximately 5 to 8 teaspoons of fat and oils per day for cooking, baking, salads and spreads.
- Use cooking methods that require little or no fat: boil, broil, bake, roast, poach and steam.
- Eat no more than 3 to 4 egg *yolks* per week, including those used in cooking, baking and in store-bought baked goods. (Egg whites are okay.)

- Limit your intake of organ meats, such as liver, brains, chitterlings, kidney, heart, gizzard, sweetbreads and pork maws.
- Eat at least 5 servings of fruits and vegetables per day.
- Eat 6 or more servings of cereals and grains daily.
- Choose skim or 1% milk and low-fat dairy products.

Once you've mastered these general guidelines, you can take a look at specific foods you're eating now and make a few heart-healthy substitutions, such as replacing whole milk with skim milk, 1% milk and other low-fat dairy products.

Following is a mini-list of the kinds of foods you'll want to include in your low-fat, low-cholesterol eating plan. When planning your menus, use it as a guide to help keep your fat and cholesterol intake low.

For instance, if you're having spaghetti with meat sauce, you'll see from this guide that one cup of pasta is a serving from the bread group, the tomato sauce is from the vegetable group, and the meat is from the meat group. You may want to experiment and try adding less meat to your sauce.

By choosing a variety of foods from each group—particularly cereals and grains and fruits and vegetables—you can help build an eating plan that's low in fat and high in nutrition. It can also help keep your cholesterol level—and your risk of heart attack—on the low side.

THE AMERICAN
HEART ASSOCIATION
DIET AT A GLANCE

**MEAT, POULTRY, SEAFOOD,
DRIED BEANS AND PEAS,
AND EGGS**

Choose: the leanest cuts of
meat, poultry and
seafood. Trim all fat
before cooking.

Daily Servings: no more than 6 oz.
of lean meat, poultry
and seafood per day;
or 2 or more
servings of dried
beans and peas;
No more than 3 or 4
egg yolks a *week*
(whites are okay).

Serving Size: 3 oz. cooked (or 4
oz. raw) meat,
poultry, fish or
seafood;
1 cup cooked beans,
peas or legumes.
(Three ounces of

meat is about the size of a deck of cards, about half of a chicken breast or a leg with a thigh, or about ½ cup of flaked fish.)

VEGETABLES AND FRUITS

Choose: all vegetables and fruits except coconut. Olives and avocados are included in the fats section because of their high fat content. Oranges, grapefruit, melons and strawberries are excellent sources of vitamin C. Deep yellow fruits such as apricots and cantaloupe are high in vitamin A. Dark green vegetables such as spinach and broccoli provide vitamin C and, along with deep yellow vegetables such as

carrots, are excellent
sources of vitamin A.

Daily Servings: 5 or more.

Serving Size: 1 medium-size piece
of fruit or
½ cup fruit juice;
½ to 1 cup cooked or
raw vegetables.

BREADS, CEREALS, PASTA AND STARCHY VEGETABLES

Choose: low-fat breads, rolls,
crackers and snacks;
hot or cold cereals
(except for granola,
which may be high
in saturated fat);
homemade quick
breads made with
low-fat milk and fats
or oils low in
saturated fatty acids;
rice and pasta made
without egg.

Daily Servings: 6 or more.

Serving Size: 1 slice of bread;
¼–1 cup hot or cold
cereals;
1 cup cooked rice or
pasta;

¼–½ cup starchy
vegetables;
1 cup low-fat soup.

MILK PRODUCTS

Choose: skim or 1% milk and
low-fat cheeses.

Daily Servings: 2 or more for adults
over 24 and children
10 and under.
3–4 for ages 11–24
and women who are
pregnant or lactating.

Serving Size: 8 ounces skim or 1%
milk or yogurt;
1 ounce low-fat
cheese; ½ cup
low-fat cottage
cheese.

FATS AND OILS

Choose: vegetable oils and
margarines with no
more than 2 grams
of saturated fatty
acids per tablespoon
(canola, corn, olive,
safflower, sesame,
soybean, sunflower);
salad dressings and

mayonnaise with no
more than 1 gram of
saturated fatty acids
per tablespoon.

Daily Servings: 5 to 8, depending on
your caloric needs.

Serving Size: 1 tsp. vegetable oil
or regular margarine;
2 tsp. diet
margarine, salad
dressing,
mayonnaise or
peanut butter;
3 tsp. seeds, nuts,
chopped avocados
or olives.

DESSERTS

Choose: desserts low in
saturated fatty acids,
cholesterol and
calories.
You can also make
your own desserts
by using ingredients
from the above lists.

SNACKS

Choose: snacks from other
food groups: fruits,

raw vegetables and dips, nutritious cookies, low-fat crackers and pretzels, seeds and nuts, etc.

BEVERAGES

Choose: fruit or vegetable juices, coffee, tea, mineral water. If you drink, have no more than 1 ounce ethanol per day, which is about 2 drinks of wine, beer or liquor. If you don't drink, don't start.

HOW TO USE
THIS GUIDE

A Cholesterol Counter
You Can Count On

THIS low-fat way of eating is easy, but there are so many food products to choose from, it can get confusing. The hardest thing about cutting down on cholesterol, calories, sodium and the like is knowing which foods provide what nutrients.

That's why the American Heart Association prepared this *Fat and Cholesterol Counter*. It offers more than 450 foods, listing amounts of the following nutrients contained in each: total fat, saturated fatty acids, calories, cholesterol and sodium. The section on fats and oils also lists polyunsaturated fatty acids.

With these tables, you can select healthful, nutritious, low-fat, low-sodium foods that can help keep your weight down, your cholesterol level low and your heart healthy.

Figuring Your Fat Allowance

THE first step is to determine the maximum amount of fat you can eat every day—and still keep your blood cholesterol at a safe level.

To discover this, you must first know how many calories you need to maintain your ideal weight. Here's an easy way to find the *approximate* number of calories you'll need. It is simply a guide. People who are very active will need more calories. Children and pregnant and lactating women have special caloric needs. Ask your physician to guide you. Start by finding your ideal weight in the table opposite.

DESIRABLE BODY WEIGHT RANGES

HEIGHT WITHOUT SHOES	WEIGHT WITHOUT CLOTHES	
(ft./in.)	Men (pounds)	Women (pounds)
4'10"	—	92–121
4'11"	—	95–124
5'0"	—	98–127
5'1"	105–134	101–130
5'2"	108–137	104–134
5'3"	111–141	107–138
5'4"	114–145	110–142
5'5"	117–149	114–146
5'6"	121–154	118–150
5'7"	125–159	122–154
5'8"	129–163	126–159
5'9"	133–167	130–164
5'10"	137–172	134–169
5'11"	141–177	—
6'0"	145–182	—
6'1"	149–187	—
6'2"	153–192	—
6'3"	157–197	—

This table is adapted from the Desirable Weight Table prepared in 1959 by the Metropolitan Life Insurance Company. It is based on weights for small, medium, and large frames associated with the lowest mortality. To arrive at the normal weight for women 18 to 25, subtract 1 pound for each year under 25.

The 1983 revision of the Metropolitan Life Insurance Company's Height and Weight Tables permitted a greater weight for some heights. However, because obesity is a contributing factor for heart disease, the American Heart Association did not adapt the 1983 version.

Next, to find your caloric needs, multiply your ideal weight by 15 if you're moderately active or 20 if you are very active. From that total, subtract the following numbers according to your age:

Age 25 to 34, subtract 0
Age 35 to 44, subtract 100
Age 45 to 54, subtract 200
Age 55 to 64, subtract 300
Age 65+, subtract 400

For example, if you're a forty-five-year-old man whose desirable weight is 145 pounds and who is moderately active, take 145 lb., multiply by 15 to get 2,175 calories; then subtract 200 to get 1,975 calories. For a moderately active 120-pound thirty-five-year-old woman, you'd figure it like this: $120 \times 15 = 1,800 - 100 = 1,700$.

After you figure how many calories you need, you can determine the maximum amount of fat that should be in your diet. At the American Heart Association, we recommend that your total fat intake be no more than 30 percent of your total calories. And we suggest keeping saturated fatty acids to 10 percent or less of total calories.

To find out how many grams of fat you can allow yourself, take your daily calories and multiply by .30. That will give you the daily calories you can have from fat. Then divide that number by 9, which will give you the number of total grams of fat you can have each day. For example, 2,000 calories × .30 = 600 ÷ 9 = 67 grams of total fat. Remember that total fat is made up of saturated, polyunsaturated and mono-unsaturated fatty acids.

Then you do the same thing with saturated fatty acids. Total calories multiplied by .10, then divided by 9. Example: 2,000 × .10 ÷ 9 = 22 grams of saturated fatty acids. The table on page 22 shows the maximum grams of total fat and saturated fatty acids for a variety of calorie levels.

SUGGESTED DAILY FAT INTAKE

Daily Calories	Maximum Grams of Total Fat	Maximum Grams of Saturated Fatty Acids
1,200	40	13
1,400	47	16
1,600	53	18
1,800	60	20
2,000	67	22
2,200	73	24
2,400	80	27
2,600	87	29
2,800	93	31
3,000	100	33

Check food labels on prepared foods to see how many grams of fat are in one serving of the product. The grams of fat are listed under "Nutrition Information Per Serving" on any package that provides a nutrition label. For example, the label opposite shows 5 grams of fat in each 4-ounce portion of spaghetti sauce.

SPAGHETTI SAUCE

NUTRITION
INFORMATION
PER SERVING

Serving Size	4 ounces
	(113 grams)
Servings Per Container	7⅞
Calories	130
Protein (grams)	2
Carbohydrate (grams)	18
Fat (grams)	5

Just keep track of the number of grams of total fat and saturated fatty acids you eat every day. You will then see if your intake of fat and saturated fatty acids is within the guidelines listed on the chart opposite. If not, adjust your eating so that it will fall within the guidelines.

Getting the Most from the Fat and Cholesterol Counter

YOU'LL find all kinds of everyday foods listed in the following Food Table. Some are more nutritious and lower in fat than others. We've tried to list all the choices available to you in real life: the healthful and the not so healthful. By comparing the nutrients in these foods you will quickly learn the flavorful, lower-fat substitutes you can make.

If you're following our AHA diet guidelines, you'll see that our basic 1,600-calorie eating plan will give you all the nutrients you need. Then if you need to add calories, select additional foods from all the food groups except Meat, Poultry, Seafood and Eggs.

You'll find that when you stick as closely as possible to low-fat, low-cholesterol foods, you can splurge once in a while on one of the high-fat foods listed here—with no ill effects! For the rest of the day or the next day, balance your fat intake by selecting low-fat items. We included high-fat foods in our table, not so that you will eat them, but to show you how much higher they are in saturated fatty acids and cholesterol when compared with wholesome low-fat foods. When the desire for a high-fat dessert overtakes you, here's something that works for lots of people: Eat a small serving or share it with your dining partner or partners.

How to Read the Food Table

THE Food Table is lengthy, but it's easy to understand. The foods are listed in categories, and the amount of foods analyzed is listed also.

The table offers the following information on each food: total weight in grams, grams of total fat and saturated fatty acids, number of calories, and milligrams of cholesterol and sodium. In the Fats and Oils section, polyunsaturated fat is also listed in grams. When you see a dash (—) in the table, it means that information was not available on that item. When foods have only a small amount of a given nutrient, the table reads "tr," for "trace." The

Food Table was prepared using data from the USDA Handbooks listed on page 103.

It's easy to use these tables to help plan your daily menu so that you won't exceed your allotted grams of total fat. For example, suppose your daily calories are 1,200, which allows you 40 grams of total fat. Reading the table, you'll see that if you eat gourmet ice cream, you'll take in almost 12 grams of fat, leaving you only 28 grams. On the other hand, if you choose orange sherbet, you'll use only 2 of your 40 grams. Also, ice cream would use more than half of your allowance of saturated fatty acids. Sherbet uses less than one-tenth of the total.

The important thing is to include the recommended numbers of servings from all food groups in the basic plan. Then you will get all the vitamins and minerals your body needs.

The truth is, choice is everything.

Compare the total fat levels in these food choices: An apple turnover at a fast-food restaurant has 14 grams of fat; a plain apple has less than half a gram. A 4-ounce fast-food cheeseburger has 31 grams of fat; a tuna sandwich has about 12. Three ounces of lean broiled rib-eye steak has about 10 grams of fat; three ounces of top sirloin, trimmed of all fat, has about 5. Three ounces of halibut has about 3 grams of fat. A brownie with nuts and frosting has about 13 grams of fat; four raisin oatmeal cookies made with oil and egg whites have 9 grams. Notice that the fat content of food depends on the food itself *and* the way it is cooked. In the case of meat, it also depends on the grade and fat trim.

Armed with this table, you can eat foods you enjoy and keep your blood cholesterol level low at the same time.

Here's to good eating—and good health!

KEY DEFINITIONS

ATHEROSCLEROSIS▪A blood vessel disease where the inner linings of arteries become thick and irregular due to deposits of fat, cholesterol and other substances. These arteries then become narrowed and the flow of blood to the heart is reduced.

CALORIE▪The unit of measurement of the heat or energy supplied by food when it is broken down in the body. Carbohydrates, protein, fat and alcohol supply calories.

CHOLESTEROL▪A fat-like substance produced by your body and contained in foods of animal origin only. Your body produces all the cholesterol it needs. The cholesterol from foods can raise your blood cholesterol level, and, thus increase your risk of heart disease. Cholesterol is found in egg yolks, organ meats, meats, fish, seafood, poultry and dairy products.

HYDROGENATED FAT· This type of fat results from a chemical process that changes a liquid oil that is naturally high in unsaturated fats to a more solid and more saturated form. This process helps the fat in food products stay fresh longer. The greater the degree of hydrogenation, the more saturated the fat becomes. Hydrogenated margarines and spreads are acceptable if they contain no more than 2 grams of saturated fatty acids per tablespoon.

MONOUNSATURATED FATTY ACIDS· Fats that are found in canola, olive and peanut oils. They are also found in foods such as meats, nuts and seeds. Like polyunsaturated fatty acids, monounsaturated fatty acids tend to lower blood cholesterol, especially when they're used to replace saturated fatty acids in the diet.

POLYUNSATURATED FATTY ACIDS· Fats such as safflower, sunflower, corn and soybean. They are also found in foods such as nuts and seeds. They tend to lower blood cholesterol when they are used as part of a low-saturated fat, low-cholesterol eating plan.

SATURATED FATTY ACIDS ▪ The main culprit in raising blood cholesterol. Saturated fatty acids are found in both animal and plant foods. Animal foods containing large amounts of saturated fatty acids include beef, veal, lamb, pork and ham, butter, cream, whole milk, cheese and dairy products made from whole milk. The plant soures of saturated fatty acids include coconut oil, cocoa butter, palm and palm kernel oil and some shortenings and margarines. Many commercial baked goods are made with these oils.

SODIUM ▪ A mineral that is essential for good health. The body only needs a tiny amount each day. Most foods in their natural state contain small amounts of sodium. Table salt (sodium chloride) is 40% sodium by weight. Most Americans consume far more sodium than their bodies need. In some people, this can contribute to high blood pressure.

AMERICAN HEART ASSOCIATION

FOOD TABLES

FOOD DESCRIPTION/ PORTION	Wt. Gm	Tot. Fat Gm	Sat. Fat Gm	Cal.	Chol. Mg	Sod. Mg
MEAT, POULTRY AND SEAFOOD						
Finfish						
Catfish, breaded and fried (3 oz.)	84	11.4	2.7	195	69	237
Cod, Atlantic, cooked, dry heat (3 oz.)	84	0.6	0.3	90	48	66
Eel, cooked, dry heat (3 oz.)	84	12.6	2.7	201	138	54
Fish Sticks and portions, frozen and reheated (3 oz.)	84	10.2	2.7	228	93	489
Flounder, cooked, dry heat (3 oz.)	84	1.2	0.3	99	57	90
Grouper, cooked, dry heat (3 oz.)	84	1.2	0.3	99	39	45
Haddock, cooked, dry heat (3 oz.)	84	0.9	0.3	96	63	75

FOOD DESCRIPTION/ PORTION	Wt. Gm	Tot. Fat Gm	Sat. Fat Gm	Cal.	Chol. Mg	Sod. Mg
Halibut, cooked, dry heat (3 oz.)	84	2.4	0.3	120	36	60
Herring, pickled (3 oz.)	84	15.3	2.1	222	12	741
Mackerel, canned, drained solids (3 oz.)	84	5.4	1.5	132	66	321
Mackerel, cooked, dry heat (3 oz.)	84	15.0	3.6	222	63	72
Ocean Perch, cooked, dry heat (3 oz.)	84	1.8	0.3	102	45	81
Perch, cooked, dry heat (3 oz.)	84	0.9	0.3	99	99	66
Pike, Northern, cooked, dry (3 oz.)	84	0.9	tr	96	42	42
Pollack, Walleye, cooked, dry heat (3 oz.)	84	0.9	0.3	96	81	99
Pompano, cooked, dry heat (3 oz.)	84	10.2	3.9	180	54	66

FOOD DESCRIPTION/ PORTION	Wt. Gm	Tot. Fat Gm	Sat. Fat Gm	Cal.	Chol. Mg	Sod. Mg
Redfish (see Ocean Perch)						
Rockfish, cooked, dry heat (3 oz.)	84	1.8	0.3	102	39	66
Salmon, Chinook, smoked (3 oz.)	84	3.6	0.9	99	21	660*
Salmon, Chum, canned, drained solids with bone (3 oz.)	84	4.8	1.2	120	33	414**
Salmon, Coho, cooked, moist heat (3 oz.)	84	6.3	1.2	156	42	51
Salmon, Sockeye, canned, drained solids with bone (3 oz.)	84	6.3	1.5	129	36	459**

* Regular lox has approximately 567 mg. sodium per ounce.
** With added salt.

FOOD DESCRIPTION/ PORTION	Wt. Gm	Tot. Fat Gm	Sat. Fat Gm	Cal.	Chol. Mg	Sod. Mg
Sardine, Atlantic, canned in oil, drained solids with bone (3 oz.)	84	9.6	tr	177	120	429
Sardine, Pacific, canned in tomato sauce, drained solids with bone (3 oz.)	84	10.2	2.7	150	51	351
Scrod (see Cod, page 33)						
Sea Bass, cooked, dry heat (3 oz.)	84	2.1	0.6	105	45	75
Snapper, cooked, dry heat (3 oz.)	84	1.5	0.3	108	39	48
Sole (see Flounder)						
Swordfish, cooked, dry heat (3 oz.)	84	4.5	1.2	132	42	99
Trout, Rainbow, cooked, dry heat (3 oz.)	84	3.6	0.6	129	63	30

FOOD DESCRIPTION/ PORTION	Wt. Gm	Tot. Fat Gm	Sat. Fat Gm	Cal.	Chol. Mg	Sod. Mg
Tuna, light, canned in oil, drained solids (3 oz.)	84	6.9	1.2	168	15	300
Tuna, light, canned in water, drained solids (3 oz.)	84	0.3	0.3	111	—	303
Tuna, white, canned in oil, drained solids (3 oz.)	84	6.9	—	159	27	336
Tuna, white, canned in water, drained solids (3 oz.)	84	2.1	0.6	117	36	333
Tuna Salad, prepared with light tuna in oil, pickle relish, salad dressing, onion, celery (½ cup)	103	9.5	1.6	192	14	412

FOOD DESCRIPTION/ PORTION	Wt. Gm	Tot. Fat Gm	Sat. Fat Gm	Cal.	Chol. Mg	Sod. Mg
Shellfish						
Clams, cooked, moist heat (3 oz.)	84	1.8	0.3	126	57	96
Crab, Alaskan King, cooked, moist heat (3 oz.)	84	1.2	tr	81	45	912
Crab, Alaskan King, imitation, made from surimi (3 oz.)	84	1.2	—	87	18	714
Crab, Blue, cooked, moist heat (3 oz.)	84	1.5	0.3	87	84	237
Crab Cakes, prepared with egg, fried in margarine (3 oz.)	90	6.8	1.4	140	135	297
Crayfish, cooked, moist heat (3 oz.)	84	1.2	0.3	96	150	57
Lobster, Northern, cooked, moist heat (3 oz.)	84	0.6	tr	84	60	324

FOOD DESCRIPTION/ PORTION	Wt. Gm	Tot. Fat Gm	Sat. Fat Gm	Cal.	Chol. Mg	Sod. Mg
Oysters, Eastern, breaded and fried (3 oz.)	84	10.8	2.7	168	69	354
Scallops, breaded and fried (6 large)	93	10.2	2.4	201	57	432
Shrimp, breaded and fried (12 large)	90	11.1	1.8	219	159	309
Shrimp, cooked (3 oz.)	84	0.9	0.3	84	165	189
Shrimp, imitation, made from surimi (3 oz.)	94	1.2	—	87	30	600

Chicken

Light Meat, without skin, stewed (3 oz.)	84	3.3	0.9	135	66	54
Light Meat, with skin, stewed (3 oz.)	84	8.4	2.4	171	63	54
Dark Meat, without skin, stewed (3 oz.)	84	7.5	2.1	162	75	63

FOOD DESCRIPTION/ PORTION	Wt. Gm	Tot. Fat Gm	Sat. Fat Gm	Cal.	Chol. Mg	Sod. Mg
Dark Meat, with skin, stewed (3 oz.)	84	12.6	4.8	198	69	60
Breast, half, meat only, stewed (3 oz.)	95	2.9	0.8	144	73	59
Breast, half, meat and skin, stewed (4 oz.)	110	8.2	2.3	202	83	68
Breast, half, meat and skin, fried with batter (5 oz.)	140	18.5	4.9	364	119	385
Drumstick, meat only, stewed (1½ oz.)	46	2.6	0.7	78	40	37
Drumstick, meat and skin, stewed (2 oz.)	57	6.1	1.7	116	48	43
Drumstick, meat and skin, fried with batter (2½ oz.)	72	11.3	3.0	193	62	194
Thigh, meat only, stewed (2 oz.)	55	5.4	1.5	107	49	41
Thigh, meat and skin, stewed (2½ oz.)	68	10.0	2.8	158	57	49

FOOD DESCRIPTION/ PORTION	Wt. Gm	Tot. Fat Gm	Sat. Fat Gm	Cal.	Chol. Mg	Sod. Mg
Thigh, meat and skin, fried with batter (3 oz.)	86	14.2	3.8	238	80	248
Wing, meat only, stewed (1 oz.)	24	1.7	0.5	43	18	18
Wing, meat and skin, stewed (1½ oz.)	40	6.7	1.9	100	28	27
Wing, meat and skin, fried with batter (1¾ oz.)	49	10.7	2.9	159	39	157
Boneless, canned in broth (3 oz.)	84	6.6	1.8	141	186	429
Frankfurter, chicken (3 oz.)	84	16.5	4.8	219	84	1164
Giblets— gizzard, heart, liver (1 each) (2½ oz.)	68	3.6	1.1	112	243	40
Giblets— gizzard, heart, liver (3 oz.)	84	4.5	1.5	141	303	51
Liver Pâté, canned (6 Tbsp.)	84	11.1	—	171	—	—
Chicken Roll, light (3 oz.)	84	6.3	1.8	135	42	498

FOOD DESCRIPTION/ PORTION	Wt. Gm	Tot. Fat Gm	Sat. Fat Gm	Cal.	Chol. Mg	Sod. Mg
Spread, canned (3 oz.)	84	9.9	—	165	—	—
Turkey						
Light Meat, meat only, roasted (3 oz.)	84	0.9	0.3	120	72	48
Light Meat, meat and skin, roasted (3 oz.)	84	7.2	2.1	138	66	54
Dark Meat, meat only, roasted (3 oz.)	84	3.6	1.2	138	96	66
Dark Meat, meat and skin, roasted (3 oz.)	84	9.9	3.0	189	75	66
Turkey Ham, cured, thigh meat (3 oz.)	84	4.2	1.5	111	—	849
Turkey Pastrami (3 oz.)	84	5.4	1.5	120	—	891
Turkey Roll, light and dark meat (3 oz.)	84	6.0	1.8	126	48	498
Turkey, frozen with gravy, 1 package (15 oz.)	426	11.1	3.6	285	—	2358

FOOD DESCRIPTION/ PORTION	Wt. Gm	Tot. Fat Gm	Sat. Fat Gm	Cal.	Chol. Mg	Sod. Mg
Turkey, frozen with gravy (3 oz.)	84	2.4	0.6	57	—	471
Giblets— gizzard, heart, liver (1 each) (5½ oz.)	158	8.0	2.4	264	660	92
Giblets— gizzard, heart, liver (3 oz.)	84	4.2	1.2	141	357	51
Young Toms, meat only, roasted (3 oz.)	84	3.9	1.3	141	65	62
Young Toms, light meat without skin, roasted (3 oz.)	84	2.4	0.8	129	58	57
Beef						
Arm Pot Roast, choice, lean only, trimmed to 0″ fat, braised (3 oz.)	85	7.4	2.7	187	86	56
Arm Pot Roast, choice, lean only, trimmed to ¼″ fat, braised (3 oz.)	85	7.9	2.9	191	86	56

FOOD DESCRIPTION/ PORTION	Wt. Gm	Tot. Fat Gm	Sat. Fat Gm	Cal.	Chol. Mg	Sod. Mg
Arm Pot Roast, select, lean only, trimmed to 0″ fat, braised (3 oz.)	85	5.4	1.9	168	86	56
Arm Pot Roast, select, lean only, trimmed to ¼″ fat, braised (3 oz.)	85	6.1	2.2	175	86	56
Blade Roast, choice, !ean and fat, trimmed to ¼″ fat, braised (3 oz.)	85	23.7	9.3	309	88	54
Blade Roast, choice, lean only, trimmed to 0″ fat, braised (3 oz.)	85	12.5	4.9	225	90	60
Blade Roast, choice, lean only, trimmed to ¼″ fat, braised (3 oz.)	85	12.2	4.8	223	90	60

FOOD DESCRIPTION/ PORTION	Wt. Gm	Tot. Fat Gm	Sat. Fat Gm	Cal.	Chol. Mg	Sod. Mg
Bottom Round, choice, lean only, trimmed to 0" fat, braised (3 oz.)	85	7.4	2.5	181	82	43
Bottom Round, choice, lean only, trimmed to ¼" fat, braised (3 oz.)	85	8.0	2.7	187	82	43
Bottom Round, choice, lean only, trimmed to 0" fat, roasted (3 oz.)	85	6.6	2.2	164	66	56
Bottom Round, choice, lean only, trimmed to ¼" fat, roasted (3 oz.)	85	7.1	2.4	168	66	56
Bottom Round, select, lean only, trimmed to 0" fat, braised (3 oz.)	85	5.4	1.8	163	82	43
Bottom Round, select, lean only, trimmed to ¼" fat, braised (3 oz.)	85	5.8	2.0	167	82	43

FOOD DESCRIPTION/ PORTION	Wt. Gm	Tot. Fat Gm	Sat. Fat Gm	Cal.	Chol. Mg	Sod. Mg
Bottom Round, select, lean only, trimmed to 0" fat, roasted (3 oz.)	85	4.6	1.5	146	66	56
Bottom Round, select, lean only, trimmed to ¼" fat, roasted (3 oz.)	85	5.3	1.8	152	66	56
Eye of Round, choice, lean only, trimmed to 0" fat, roasted (3 oz.)	85	4.8	1.8	149	59	53
Eye of Round, select, lean only, trimmed to 0" fat, roasted (3 oz.)	85	3.0	1.1	132	59	53
Eye of Round, select, lean only, trimmed to ¼" fat, roasted (3 oz.)	85	3.4	1.2	136	59	53
Flank, choice, lean only, trimmed to 0" fat, broiled (3 oz.)	85	8.7	3.6	177	57	70

FOOD DESCRIPTION/ PORTION	Wt. Gm	Tot. Fat Gm	Sat. Fat Gm	Cal.	Chol. Mg	Sod. Mg
Ground, extra lean, broiled, medium (3 oz.)	85	13.9	5.5	217	71	59
Ground, lean, broiled, medium (3 oz.)	85	15.7	6.2	231	74	65
Ground, regular, broiled, medium (3 oz.)	85	17.7	6.9	246	76	70
Heart, simmered (3 oz.)	85	4.8	1.5	147	165	54
Kidney, simmered (3 oz.)	85	3.0	0.9	123	330	114
Liver, braised (3 oz.)	85	4.2	1.5	138	330	90
Rib, large end (ribs 6–9), choice, lean only, trimmed to 0" fat, roasted (3 oz.)	85	12.9	5.1	216	69	62

FOOD DESCRIPTION/ PORTION	Wt. Gm	Tot. Fat Gm	Sat. Fat Gm	Cal.	Chol. Mg	Sod. Mg
Rib, large end (ribs 6–9), choice, lean and fat, trimmed to 0" fat, roasted (3 oz.)	85	26.0	10.5	317	72	54
Rib, large end (ribs 6–9), choice, lean and fat, trimmed to ¼" fat, roasted (3 oz.)	85	27.3	11.1	327	73	54
Rib, small end (ribs 10–12), choice, lean only, trimmed to 0" fat, broiled (3 oz.)	85	9.9	3.9	192	68	59
Rib, small end (ribs 10–12), choice, lean only, trimmed to ¼" fat, broiled (3 oz.)	85	10.7	4.3	198	68	59

FOOD DESCRIPTION/ PORTION	Wt. Gm	Tot. Fat Gm	Sat. Fat Gm	Cal.	Chol. Mg	Sod. Mg
Rib, small end (ribs 10–12), choice, lean and fat, trimmed to ¼" fat, broiled (3 oz.)	85	23.4	9.6	297	71	52
Rib, small end, select, lean only, trimmed to 0" fat, broiled (3 oz.)	85	7.4	3.0	168	68	59
Rib, small end, select, lean only, trimmed to ¼" fat, broiled (3 oz.)	85	8.2	3.3	176	68	59
Rib, whole, select, lean only, trimmed to ¼" fat, broiled (3 oz.)	85	8.9	3.6	175	66	60
T-Bone Steak, choice, lean only, trimmed to ¼" fat, broiled (3 oz.)	85	8.8	3.5	182	68	56

FOOD DESCRIPTION/ PORTION	Wt. Gm	Tot. Fat Gm	Sat. Fat Gm	Cal.	Chol. Mg	Sod. Mg
Tenderloin, choice, lean only, trimmed to 0" fat, broiled (3 oz.)	85	8.6	3.2	180	71	54
Tenderloin, choice, lean only, trimmed to ¼" fat, broiled (3 oz.)	85	9.5	3.6	188	71	54
Tenderloin, select, lean only, trimmed to 0" fat, broiled (3 oz.)	85	7.5	2.8	170	71	54
Tip Round, choice, lean only, trimmed to 0" fat, roasted (3 oz.)	85	5.4	1.9	153	69	55
Tip Round, choice, lean only, trimmed to ¼" fat, roasted (3 oz.)	85	6.2	2.2	160	69	55

FOOD DESCRIPTION/ PORTION	Wt. Gm	Tot. Fat Gm	Sat. Fat Gm	Cal.	Chol. Mg	Sod. Mg
Tip Round, select, lean and fat, trimmed to 0" fat, roasted (3 oz.)	85	6.2	2.3	158	69	55
Tip Round, select, lean only, trimmed to ¼" fat, roasted (3 oz.)	85	5.4	1.9	153	69	55
Tongue, simmered (3 oz.)	85	17.7	7.5	240	90	51
Top Loin, choice, lean only, trimmed to 0" fat, broiled (3 oz.)	85	8.2	3.1	177	65	58
Top Loin, choice, lean only, trimmed to ¼" fat, broiled (3 oz.)	85	8.6	3.3	182	65	58
Top Loin, select, lean only, trimmed to 0" fat, broiled (3 oz.)	85	5.9	2.2	157	65	58

FOOD DESCRIPTION/ PORTION	Wt. Gm	Tot. Fat Gm	Sat. Fat Gm	Cal.	Chol. Mg	Sod. Mg
Top Loin, select, lean only, trimmed to ¼" fat, broiled (3 oz.)	85	6.6	2.5	164	65	58
Top Round, choice, lean only, trimmed to 0" fat, braised (3 oz.)	85	4.9	1.7	176	76	38
Top Round, choice, lean only, trimmed to ¼" fat, braised (3 oz.)	85	5.5	1.9	181	76	38
Top Round, choice, lean only, trimmed to ¼" fat, broiled (3 oz.)	85	5.0	1.7	160	71	52
Top Round, choice, lean only, trimmed to ¼" fat, pan-fried (3 oz.)	85	7.3	2.1	193	82	60
Top Round, select, lean only, trimmed to 0" fat, braised (3 oz.)	85	3.4	1.2	162	76	38

FOOD DESCRIPTION/ PORTION	Wt. Gm	Tot. Fat Gm	Sat. Fat Gm	Cal.	Chol. Mg	Sod. Mg
Top Round, select, lean only, trimmed to ¼" fat, braised (3 oz.)	85	3.9	1.3	166	76	38
Top Round, select, lean only, trimmed to ¼" fat, broiled (3 oz.)	85	3.1	1.1	143	71	52
Top Sirloin, choice, lean only, trimmed to 0" fat, broiled (3 oz.)	85	6.6	2.6	170	76	56
Top Sirloin, choice, lean only, trimmed to ¼" fat, broiled (3 oz.)	85	6.8	2.7	172	76	56
Top Sirloin, select, lean only, trimmed to 0" fat, broiled (3 oz)	85	4.8	1.9	153	76	56
Top Sirloin, select, lean only, trimmed to ¼" fat, broiled (3 oz.)	85	5.3	2.1	158	76	56
Tripe (3 oz.)	85	3.3	1.8	84	81	39

FOOD DESCRIPTION/ PORTION	Wt. Gm	Tot. Fat Gm	Sat. Fat Gm	Cal.	Chol. Mg	Sod. Mg
Veal						
Arm Steak, lean only, braised (3 oz.)	84	4.5	1.2	171	132	75
Average, all grades, lean only, cooked (3 oz.)	84	5.7	1.5	165	99	75
Blade Steak, lean only, braised (3 oz.)	84	5.4	1.5	168	135	87
Loin Chop, lean only, braised (3 oz.)	84	6.0	2.1	150	90	81
Rib Roast, lean only, cooked (3 oz.)	84	6.3	1.8	150	96	81
Lamb						
Average, all grades, lean only, cooked (3 oz.)	84	8.1	3.0	174	78	63
Foreshank, lean only, braised (3 oz.)	84	5.1	1.8	159	90	63

FOOD DESCRIPTION/ PORTION	Wt. Gm	Tot. Fat Gm	Sat. Fat Gm	Cal.	Chol. Mg	Sod. Mg
Leg, shank portion, lean only, roasted (3 oz.)	84	5.7	2.1	153	75	57
Loin Chops, lean only, broiled (3 oz.)	84	8.4	1.8	183	81	72
Rack, rib, lean only, roasted (3 oz.)	84	11.4	3.9	198	75	69

Pork

FOOD DESCRIPTION/ PORTION	Wt. Gm	Tot. Fat Gm	Sat. Fat Gm	Cal.	Chol. Mg	Sod. Mg
Bacon, pan-fried, 4½ slices (1 oz.)	28	14.0	5.0	163	24	452
Canadian Bacon, grilled (3 oz.)	84	7.2	2.4	156	48	1314
Chitterlings, simmered (3 oz.)	84	24.6	8.7	258	123	33
Fresh Pork, center loin, lean only, broiled (3 oz.)	84	9.0	3.0	195	84	66

FOOD DESCRIPTION/ PORTION	Wt. Gm	Tot. Fat Gm	Sat. Fat Gm	Cal.	Chol. Mg	Sod. Mg
Fresh Pork, arm, picnic, shoulder, lean only, roasted (3 oz.)	84	10.8	3.6	195	81	69
Fresh Pork, shoulder, blade, Boston, lean only, roasted (3 oz.)	84	14.4	4.8	219	84	63
Fresh Pork, sirloin, lean only, broiled (3 oz.)	84	11.7	3.9	207	84	51
Fresh Pork, tenderloin, lean only, roasted (3 oz.)	84	4.2	1.5	141	78	57
Fresh Pork, whole leg, lean only, roasted (3 oz.)	84	9.3	3.3	186	81	54
Ham, boneless, canned, extra lean, roasted (3 oz.)	84	4.2	1.5	117	24	966

FOOD DESCRIPTION/ PORTION	Wt. Gm	Tot. Fat Gm	Sat. Fat Gm	Cal.	Chol. Mg	Sod. Mg
Ham, boneless, canned, regular, roasted (3 oz.)	84	12.9	4.2	192	51	801
Ham, boneless, extra lean, roasted (3 oz.)	84	4.8	1.5	123	45	1023
Liver, braised (3 oz.)	84	3.9	1.2	141	303	42
Spareribs, lean and fat, braised (3 oz.)	84	25.8	9.9	339	102	78
Game						
Deer (Venison), roasted (3 oz.)	85	2.7	1.1	134	95	46
Goose, domesticated, meat only, roasted (3 oz.)	84	10.8	3.9	201	78	60
Goose, domesticated, meat and skin, roasted (3 oz.)	84	18.6	6.0	258	78	60
Rabbit, domesticated, stewed (3 oz.)	85	7.2	2.1	175	73	31

FOOD DESCRIPTION/ PORTION	Wt. Gm	Tot. Fat Gm	Sat. Fat Gm	Cal.	Chol. Mg	Sod. Mg
Luncheon Meat and Sausage						
Bologna, beef and pork (3 oz.)	84	24.0	9.0	267	48	867
Braunschweiger, pork (3 oz.)	84	27.3	9.3	306	132	972
Chicken Spread, canned (6 Tbsp.)	78	9.9	—	165	—	—
Frankfurter, beef and pork (3 oz.)	84	24.9	9.3	273	42	954
Frankfurter, chicken (3 oz.)	84	16.5	4.8	219	84	1164
Pepperoni, pork, beef (3 oz.)	84	37.5	13.8	423	—	1734
Salad Spread, ham, cured (6 Tbsp.)	90	14.1	4.5	192	36	822
Salami, dry, pork, beef (3 oz.)	84	29.4	10.5	357	66	1581
Sausage, Italian, pork, cooked (3 oz.)	84	21.9	7.8	276	66	783

FOOD DESCRIPTION/ PORTION	Wt. Gm	Tot. Fat Gm	Sat. Fat Gm	Cal.	Chol. Mg	Sod. Mg
Sausage, knockwurst, pork, beef (3 oz.)	84	23.7	8.7	261	48	858
Sausage, liverwurst, pork (3 oz.)	84	24.3	9.0	279	135	732
Sausage, Polish, pork (3 oz.)	84	24.3	8.7	276	60	744
Sausage, pork, fresh, cooked (3 oz.)	84	26.4	9.3	315	72	1098
Sausage, Vienna, beef and pork, canned (4½ links)	84	21.3	7.8	237	45	810

Mixed Dishes with Meat, Poultry and Seafood

Chicken à la King (1 cup)	245	34.3	12.9	468	220	760
Chicken and Noodle Casserole (1 cup)	240	18.5	5.9	367	—	600

FOOD DESCRIPTION/ PORTION	Wt. Gm	Tot. Fat Gm	Sat. Fat Gm	Cal.	Chol. Mg	Sod. Mg
Chili con Carne, with beans, canned (1 cup)	255	14.0	6.0	286	—	1330
Chop Suey, beef and pork, without noodles (1 cup)	250	17.0	8.5	300	—	1053
Chow Mein, chicken, without noodles (1 cup)	250	10.0	2.4	255	—	718
Macaroni and Cheese, canned (1 cup)	240	9.6	4.2	228	—	730
Macaroni and Cheese, homemade (1 cup)	200	22.2	11.9	430	—	1086
Pâté, chicken liver (½ cup)	104	13.6	—	208	—	0
Pizza, cheese (⅛ of 12″ diameter)	49	2.5	1.2	109	7	261

FOOD DESCRIPTION/ PORTION	Wt. Gm	Tot. Fat Gm	Sat. Fat Gm	Cal.	Chol. Mg	Sod. Mg
Pizza, cheese, pepperoni (⅛ of 12" diameter)	53	5.2	1.7	135	11	199
Pot Pie, beef (⅓ of 9" diameter)	210	30.5	7.9	517	42	596
Pot Pie, chicken (⅓ of 9" diameter)	232	31.3	10.3	545	56	594
Spaghetti, with meatballs and tomato sauce, canned (1 cup)	250	10.8	2.2	258	—	1220
Stew, beef and vegetables (1 cup)	245	10.5	4.4	218	72	292

FOOD DESCRIPTION/ PORTION	Wt. Gm	Tot. Fat Gm	Sat. Fat Gm	Cal.	Chol. Mg	Sod. Mg
FAST FOOD						
Bacon Cheeseburger, single patty with condiments (1)	195	36.8	16.3	609	112	1044
Burrito, with beans (2)	217	13.5	6.9	448	5	986
Burrito, with beans, cheese and beef (2)	203	13.3	7.2	331	125	990
Cheeseburger, large, single meat patty, plain (1)	185	33.0	14.8	608	96	1589
Cheeseburger, large, single meat patty with condiments and vegetables (1)	219	32.9	15.0	564	88	1107
Cheeseburger, regular, single meat patty with condiments (1)	113	14.1	6.3	295	37	616

FOOD DESCRIPTION/ PORTION	Wt. Gm	Tot. Fat Gm	Sat. Fat Gm	Cal.	Chol. Mg	Sod. Mg
Chicken, breaded and fried, light meat (breast or wing) (2 pieces)	163	29.5	7.8	494	149	975
Chicken Fillet Sandwich, plain (1)	182	29.5	8.5	515	60	957
Chimichanga, with beef (1)	174	19.7	8.5	425	9	910
Cookies, animal crackers (1 box)	67	9.0	3.5	299	11	274
Eggs, scrambled (2)	94	15.2	5.8	200	400	211
Enchilada, with cheese and beef (1)	192	17.6	9.1	324	40	1320
English Muffin Sandwich with egg, cheese, Canadian bacon (1)	146	19.8	9.1	383	234	785
Fish Sandwich, with tartar sauce (1)	158	22.8	5.2	431	55	615

FOOD DESCRIPTION/ PORTION	Wt. Gm	Tot. Fat Gm	Sat. Fat Gm	Cal.	Chol. Mg	Sod. Mg
Fish Sandwich, with tartar sauce and cheese (1)	183	28.6	8.1	524	68	939
Fried Pie, apple, cherry or lemon (1)	85	14.4	6.5	266	13	325
Ham and Cheese Sandwich (1)	146	15.5	6.4	353	58	772
Hamburger, double meat, with condiments (1)	215	32.5	12.0	576	102	742
Hamburger, large, single meat patty with condi- ments and vegetables (1)	218	27.4	10.4	511	86	825
Hamburger, large, triple meat patty, plain, with condiments (1)	259	41.5	15.9	693	142	713
Hamburger, regular, single meat patty, plain (1)	90	11.8	4.1	275	36	387

FOOD DESCRIPTION/ PORTION	Wt. Gm	Tot. Fat Gm	Sat. Fat Gm	Cal.	Chol. Mg	Sod. Mg
Hamburger, regular, single meat patty with condiments and vegetables (1)	110	13.5	4.1	279	26	504
Hot Dog (1)	98	14.5	5.1	242	44	671
Hot Fudge Sundae (1)	158	8.6	5.0	284	21	182
Hush Puppies (5 pieces)	78	11.6	2.7	256	135	965
Onion Rings (8–9 rings)	83	15.5	7.0	275	14	430
Pancake, with butter and syrup (3)	232	14.0	5.9	519	57	1103
Potato, french-fried in beef tallow and vegetable oil (4 oz.)	115	18.5	7.6	358	16	187
Potato, french-fried in vegetable oil (1 regular order)	76	12.2	3.8	235	0	124
Potato Chips (10)	20	7.1	1.8	105	—	94

FOOD DESCRIPTION/ PORTION	Wt. Gm	Tot. Fat Gm	Sat. Fat Gm	Cal.	Chol. Mg	Sod. Mg
Roast Beef, on bun (1)	139	13.8	3.6	346	52	792
Shake, chocolate (10 fluid oz.)	283	10.5	6.5	360	37	273
Taco, small (1)	171	20.6	11.4	370	57	802
Tuna Salad Sub (1)	256	28.0	5.3	584	47	1294

FOOD DESCRIPTION/ PORTION	Wt. Gm	Tot. Fat Gm	Sat. Fat Gm	Cal.	Chol. Mg	Sod. Mg
EGGS						
Egg, whole, raw (1)	50	5.0	1.6	75	213	63
Egg White, raw (1)	33	tr	0	16	0	50
Egg Yolk, raw (1)	17	5.0	1.6	63	213	8
Egg, fried in butter (1)	46	6.4	2.4	83	219	144
Egg, scrambled with butter and milk (1 egg)	64	7.1	2.8	95	225	155
Egg Substitute, frozen (¼ cup)	60	6.7	1.2	96	1	120
Egg Substitute,* liquid (¼ cup)	60	2.0	0.4	50	1	106
Omelet, with butter and milk (1 egg)	64	7.1	2.8	95	225	155

* Check labels—several brands are fat-free.

FOOD DESCRIPTION/ PORTION	Wt. Gm	Tot. Fat Gm	Sat. Fat Gm	Cal.	Chol. Mg	Sod. Mg
MILK PRODUCTS						
Buttermilk, cultured (1 cup)	245	2.2	1.3	99	9	257
Condensed, sweetened, canned (1 cup)	306	26.6	16.8	982	104	389
Evaporated, skim, canned (½ cup)	128	0.3	0.2	99	5	147
Evaporated, whole, canned (½ cup)	126	9.5	5.8	169	37	133
Hot Cocoa, with whole milk (1 cup)	250	9.1	5.6	218	33	123
Malted Milk Beverage (1 cup whole milk + 4 to 5 heaping tsp. malted milk powder)	265	8.9	5.5	225	33	244
Milk, skim or nonfat (1 cup)	245	0.4	0.3	86	4	126
Milk, 1% fat (1 cup)	244	2.6	1.6	102	10	123

FOOD DESCRIPTION/ PORTION	Wt. Gm	Tot. Fat Gm	Sat. Fat Gm	Cal.	Chol. Mg	Sod. Mg
Milk, 2% fat (1 cup)	244	4.7	2.9	121	18	122
Milk, whole (1 cup)	244	8.2	5.1	150	33	120
Milk, whole, chocolate (1 cup)	250	8.5	5.3	208	30	149
Milkshake, vanilla, thick (11 oz.)	313	9.5	5.9	350	37	299

Yogurt

FOOD DESCRIPTION/ PORTION	Wt. Gm	Tot. Fat Gm	Sat. Fat Gm	Cal.	Chol. Mg	Sod. Mg
Low-fat, plain (1 cup)	227	3.5	2.3	144	14	159
Nonfat or Skim, plain (1 cup)	227	0.4	0.3	127	4	174
Whole, plain (1 cup)	227	7.4	4.8	139	29	105

Frozen Desserts

FOOD DESCRIPTION/ PORTION	Wt. Gm	Tot. Fat Gm	Sat. Fat Gm	Cal.	Chol. Mg	Sod. Mg
Frozen Yogurt (¾ cup)	170	3.5	2.3	185	14	90
Ice Cream, rich, 16% fat (¾ cup)	111	17.7	11.1	263	66	81
Ice Cream, regular, 10% fat (¾ cup)	101	10.7	6.8	203	45	87

FOOD DESCRIPTION/ PORTION	Wt. Gm	Tot. Fat Gm	Sat. Fat Gm	Cal.	Chol. Mg	Sod. Mg
Ice Milk, regular (¾ cup)	99	4.2	2.7	138	14	80
Ice Milk, soft serve (¾ cup)	132	3.5	2.1	168	11	123
Sherbet, orange (¾ cup)	146	2.9	1.8	203	11	66

Cream, Non-Dairy Creamers and Toppers

FOOD DESCRIPTION/ PORTION	Wt. Gm	Tot. Fat Gm	Sat. Fat Gm	Cal.	Chol. Mg	Sod. Mg
Creamer, non-dairy, liquid (2 Tbsp.)	30	3.0	0.6	40	0	24
Creamer, non-dairy, powder (2 tsp.)	4	1.4	1.4	22	0	8
Dessert Topping, non-dairy, frozen (2 Tbsp.)	8	2.0	1.8	26	0	2
Half-and-Half Cream (2 Tbsp.)	30	3.4	2.2	40	12	12
Sour Cream, real (2 Tbsp.)	24	5.0	3.2	52	10	12
Whipped Cream, pressurized (2 Tbsp.)	6	1.4	0.8	16	4	8

FOOD DESCRIPTION/ PORTION	Wt. Gm	Tot. Fat Gm	Sat. Fat Gm	Cal.	Chol. Mg	Sod. Mg
Whipping Cream, heavy, fluid (2 Tbsp.)	30	11.2	7.0	104	42	12
C h e e s e*						
American (1 oz.)	28	8.9	5.6	106	27	406
Blue, Brie, Cheddar, Colby, Edam, Gouda, Gruyère, Monterey, Parmesan Roquefort, Swiss (1 oz.)	28	9.4	6.0	114	30	176
Cheese Spread, process, American (1 oz.)	28	6.0	3.8	82	16	381
Cottage Cheese, creamed (½ cup)	105	4.7	3.0	109	16	425
Cottage Cheese, dry curd (½ cup)	73	0.3	0.2	62	5	10

* Many low-fat varieties are in grocery stores; check labels.

FOOD DESCRIPTION/ PORTION	Wt. Gm	Tot. Fat Gm	Sat. Fat Gm	Cal.	Chol. Mg	Sod. Mg
Cottage Cheese, low-fat, 1% (½ cup)	113	1.2	0.7	82	5	459
Cottage Cheese, low-fat, 2% (½ cup)	113	2.2	1.4	101	9	459
Cream Cheese, Neufchâtel (1 oz.)	28	6.6	4.2	74	22	113
Cream Cheese, regular (1 oz.)	28	9.9	6.2	99	31	84
Mozzarella, part skim (1 oz.)	28	4.5	2.9	72	16	132
Ricotta, part skim (1 oz.)	28	2.2	1.4	39	9	35
Ricotta, whole milk (1 oz.)	28	3.7	2.4	49	14	24

FOOD DESCRIPTION/ PORTION	Wt. Gm	Tot. Fat Gm	Sat. Fat Gm	Poly. Fat Gm	Cal.	Chol. Mg	Sod. Mg
FATS AND OILS							
Oils							
Canola (3 tsp.)	15	13.5	0.9	4.5	120	0	0
Corn (3 tsp.)	15	13.5	1.8	8.1	120	0	0
Olive (3 tsp.)	15	13.5	1.8	1.2	120	0	0
Peanut (3 tsp.)	15	13.5	2.4	4.2	120	0	0
Safflower (3 tsp.)	15	13.5	1.2	10.2	120	0	0
Sesame (3 tsp.)	15	13.5	1.8	5.7	120	0	0
Soybean (3 tsp.)	15	13.5	2.1	7.8	120	0	0
Soybean, hydrogenated (3 tsp.)	15	13.5	2.1	5.1	120	0	0
Soybean/ Cottonseed (3 tsp.)	15	13.5	2.4	6.6	120	0	0
Sunflower (3 tsp.)	15	13.5	1.5	9.0	120	0	0
Margarines							
Corn Oil, stick (3 tsp.)	15	11.4	1.8	2.4	102	0	132
Corn Oil, tub (3 tsp.)	15	11.4	2.1	4.5	102	0	153
Diet (6 tsp.)	30	11.4	1.8	4.8	99	0	276
Safflower Oil, tub (3 tsp.)	15	11.4	1.2	6.3	102	0	153

FOOD DESCRIPTION/ PORTION	Wt. Gm	Tot. Fat Gm	Sat. Fat Gm	Poly. Fat Gm	Cal.	Chol. Mg	Sod. Mg
Soybean, hydrogenated, tub (3 tsp.)	15	11.4	1.8	3.9	102	0	153
Soybean, hydrogenated, whipped, tub (3 tsp.)	15	8.7	1.8	0.9	78	0	144

Nuts
(approximately 4 ½ Tbsp.)

FOOD DESCRIPTION/ PORTION	Wt. Gm	Tot. Fat Gm	Sat. Fat Gm	Poly. Fat Gm	Cal.	Chol. Mg	Sod. Mg
Almonds, dried	42	22.2	2.1	4.7	251	0	5
Brazil Nuts, dried	42	28.2	6.9	10.4	279	0	0
Cashews, dry-roasted	42	19.8	3.9	3.3	245	0	6
Chestnuts, roasted	42	0.5	0.2	0.2	102	0	2
Coconut, flaked, sweetened	42	13.5	12.0	0.2	189	0	114
Filberts/ Hazelnuts, dried	42	26.7	2.0	2.6	269	0	2
Macadamia, oil-roasted	42	32.6	5.0	0.6	306	0	3
Mixed, dry-roasted	42	21.9	3.0	4.7	254	0	5

FOOD DESCRIPTION/ PORTION	Wt. Gm	Tot. Fat Gm	Sat. Fat Gm	Poly. Fat Gm	Cal.	Chol. Mg	Sod. Mg
Peanuts, oil-roasted	42	21.0	2.9	6.6	248	0	6
Pecans, dried	42	28.8	2.3	7.2	285	0	0
Pistachio, dry-roasted	42	22.5	2.9	3.5	258	0	3
Walnuts, Black	42	24.2	1.5	15.9	258	0	0
Walnuts, English, dried	42	26.4	2.4	16.7	273	0	5

Seeds (approximately 3 Tbsp.)

Pumpkin/ Squash, dried	42	19.5	3.8	8.9	231	0	8
Sesame, roasted and toasted	42	20.4	2.9	9.0	242	0	5
Sunflower, dried	42	21.2	2.3	14.0	243	0	2

Salad Dressing

Blue Cheese (2 Tbsp.)	30	16.0	3.0	8.6	154	0	0
French (2 Tbsp.)	32	12.8	3.0	6.8	134	0	428
Italian (2 Tbsp.)	30	14.2	2.0	8.2	138	0	232
Mayonnaise (2 Tbsp.)	28	22.0	3.2	11.4	198	16	156

FOOD DESCRIPTION/ PORTION	Wt. Gm	Tot. Fat Gm	Sat. Fat Gm	Poly. Fat Gm	Cal.	Chol. Mg	Sod. Mg
Mayonnaise-Type (2 Tbsp.)	30	9.8	1.4	5.2	114	8	208
Sandwich Spread, commercial (2 Tbsp.)	30	10.4	1.6	6.2	120	24	0
Thousand Island (2 Tbsp.)	32	11.2	1.8	6.2	118	10	218
Vinegar and Oil (2 Tbsp.)	32	16.0	3.0	7.8	144	0	0

Other Fats

FOOD DESCRIPTION/ PORTION	Wt. Gm	Tot. Fat Gm	Sat. Fat Gm	Poly. Fat Gm	Cal.	Chol. Mg	Sod. Mg
Bacon (see pg. 55)							
Butter (1 Tbsp.)	15	12.3	7.5	0.7	108	33	123
Olives, green (5 small)	17	1.8	0.2	0.2	17	0	343
Olives, ripe (2 extra large)	14	1.7	0.2	0.2	15	0	97
Peanut Butter, smooth (2 Tbsp.)	33	16.5	2.7	4.8	189	0	156
Shortening, hydrogenated soybean and cottonseed (1 Tbsp.)	12	12.9	3.3	3.3	114	0	0

FOOD DESCRIPTION/ PORTION	Wt. Gm	Tot. Fat Gm	Sat. Fat Gm	Cal.	Chol. Mg	Sod. Mg

BREADS, CEREALS, PASTA AND STARCHY VEGETABLES

Breads, Pancakes, Waffles

FOOD DESCRIPTION/ PORTION	Wt. Gm	Tot. Fat Gm	Sat. Fat Gm	Cal.	Chol. Mg	Sod. Mg
Bagel, 3″ diameter (1)	100	2.6	—	296	—	360
Biscuit, made with milk, 2″ diameter (2)	56	5.2	1.2	182	—	544
Bread, rye (2 slices)	56	2.0	—	147	—	390
Bread, wheat (2 slices)	56	2.3	—	143	—	302
Bread, white (2 slices)	46	1.8	0.4	126	—	288
Bun, hamburger, 3½″ diameter, or hot dog (1)	40	2.2	0.5	119	—	202
English Muffin, plain (1)	58	1.2	—	138	—	370
French Toast (2 slices)	130	13.4	—	306	—	514
Muffin, bran, 2″ diameter bottom (1 large)	60	5.9	1.8	156	—	269

FOOD DESCRIPTION/ PORTION	Wt. Gm	Tot. Fat Gm	Sat. Fat Gm	Cal.	Chol. Mg	Sod. Mg
Pancake, with egg, milk, 6" diameter x ½" thick (2)	110	8.0	2.9	246	—	618
Popover, 2¾" top, 2" bottom, 4" high in center (2)	60	5.6	2.0	135	—	132
Roll, hard, 3¾" diameter x 2" high (1)	50	1.6	0.4	156	—	313
Waffle, 9" x 9" x ⅝" square (1 small)	112	11.0	3.5	313	—	162

Cereals, Ready-to-Eat

FOOD DESCRIPTION/ PORTION	Wt. Gm	Tot. Fat Gm	Sat. Fat Gm	Cal.	Chol. Mg	Sod. Mg
40% Bran Flakes (1 oz.)	28	0.5	0	93	0	264
100% Bran Cereal (1 oz.)	28	0.5	—	71	0	320
Bran Squares (1 oz.)	28	0.8	—	91	0	263
Corn Flakes (1 oz.)	28	0.1	0	110	0	351
Crisp Rice, low sodium (1 oz.)	28	0.1	—	114	0	3
Granola, homemade (1 oz.)	28	7.7	1.4	138	—	3

FOOD DESCRIPTION/ PORTION	Wt. Gm	Tot. Fat Gm	Sat. Fat Gm	Cal.	Chol. Mg	Sod. Mg
Natural Cereal, with raisins and dates (1 oz.)	28	5.2	3.5	128	0	12
Puffed Wheat, plain (1 oz.)	28	0.4	0	104	0	2
Raisin Bran (1 oz.)	28	0.5	0	86	0	202
Shredded Wheat (1 large biscuit)	24	0.3	0	83	0	0
Wheat Germ, plain, toasted (1 oz.)	28	3.0	0.5	108	0	1
Wheat Nuggets (1 oz.)	28	0.1	0	101	0	197
Cereals, Cooked*						
Corn Grits, regular and quick (1 cup)	242	0.5	0.1	146	0	0
Farina, regular (1 cup)	251	0.5	0	134	0	2

* Product cooked in unsalted water.

FOOD DESCRIPTION/ PORTION	Wt. Gm	Tot. Fat Gm	Sat. Fat Gm	Cal.	Chol. Mg	Sod. Mg
Oat Bran, cooked (1 cup)	219	1.9	0.4	87	0	2
Oatmeal, cooked, regular, quick and instant (1 cup)	234	2.4	0.4	145	0	1
Pasta and Rice, Cooked						
Macaroni (¾ cup)	105	0.7	0.1	149	0	0
Noodles, chow mein (⅔ cup)	28	8.6	1.2	147	0	122
Noodles, egg (¾ cup)	141	2.1	0.4	187	47	10
Rice, brown (1 cup)	195	1.8	0.4	216	0	9
Rice, white (1 cup)	205	0.6	0.2	264	0	4
Spaghetti (1 cup)	140	0.9	0.1	197	—	0

FOOD DESCRIPTION/ PORTION	Wt. Gm	Tot. Fat Gm	Sat. Fat Gm	Cal.	Chol. Mg	Sod. Mg
Starchy Vegetables						
Corn, Lima Beans, Green Peas, Plantain, White Potato, Winter or Acorn Squash, Yam or Sweet Potato (½ cup)		0	0	80	0	*
Prepared Vegetables						
Beans, navy, cooked, boiled (½ cup)	91	0.5	0.1	129	0	1
Broadbeans, canned (½ cup)	128	0.3	0	91	0	580
Coleslaw/ Dressing with table cream (½ cup)	60	1.6	0.2	42	5	14
Corn Pudding, whole milk, egg, butter (½ cup)	125	6.6	3.2	136	115	69

* Canned vegetables are high in sodium unless the label says they are canned without salt.

FOOD DESCRIPTION/ PORTION	Wt. Gm	Tot. Fat Gm	Sat. Fat Gm	Cal.	Chol. Mg	Sod. Mg
French Fries, oven-heated, cottage-cut(17)	84	6.9	3.2	183	0	39
French Fries, fried in animal and vegetable fat (17)	84	13.9	5.7	265	10	181
Lentils, cooked, boiled (½ cup)	99	0.4	0.1	115	0	2
Onion Rings, frozen, prepared, heated in oven (7 rings)	70	18.7	6.0	285	0	263
Potato, au gratin, with whole milk, butter and cheese (⅔ cup)	168	12.8	8.0	221	40	729
Potato, hash brown (½ cup)	78	10.9	4.3	163	—	19
Potato, mashed, with whole milk and margarine (½ cup)	105	4.4	1.1	111	2	309
Potato, O'Brien, with whole milk and butter (¾ cup)	168	2.3	1.4	137	7	365

FOOD DESCRIPTION/ PORTION	Wt. Gm	Tot. Fat Gm	Sat. Fat Gm	Cal.	Chol. Mg	Sod. Mg
Potato, scalloped, with whole milk and butter (⅔ cup)	167	6.2	3.8	144	19	560
Potato, Candied Sweet Potatoes, with brown sugar, butter, 2½" x 2" piece	105	3.4	1.4	144	8	73
Potato Chips (1 oz.)	28	10.1	2.6	148	0	133
Potato Pancake, with egg, margarine (1)	76	12.6	3.4	495	93	388
Potato Puffs, vegetable oil (⅔ cup)	84	9.1	4.3	186	0	624
Potato Salad, with egg and mayonnaise (⅔ cup)	168	13.8	2.4	240	115	886
Potato Sticks (3 oz.)	84	29.4	7.5	444	0	213
Soup						
Bean, with bacon, prepared with water (1 cup)	253	5.9	1.5	173	3	952

FOOD DESCRIPTION/ PORTION	Wt. Gm	Tot. Fat Gm	Sat. Fat Gm	Cal.	Chol. Mg	Sod. Mg
Beef, chunky-style, ready-to-serve (1 cup)	240	5.1	2.6	171	14	867
Beef Broth or Bouillon, ready-to-serve (1 cup)	240	0.5	0.3	16	tr	782
Chicken, chunky-style, ready-to-serve (1 cup)	251	6.6	2.0	178	30	887
Chicken Broth, prepared with water (1 cup)	244	1.4	0.4	39	1	776
Chicken Mushroom, prepared with water (1 cup)	244	9.2	2.4	—	10	—
Chicken Noodle, prepared with water (1 cup)	241	2.5	0.7	75	7	1107
Chicken Rice, prepared with water (1 cup)	241	1.9	0.5	60	7	814
Chicken Vegetable, prepared with water (1 cup)	241	2.8	0.9	74	10	944

FOOD DESCRIPTION/ PORTION	Wt. Gm	Tot. Fat Gm	Sat. Fat Gm	Cal.	Chol. Mg	Sod. Mg
Chili Beef, prepared with water (1 cup)	250	6.6	3.3	169	12	1035
Clam Chowder, Manhattan, prepared with water (1 cup)	244	2.3	0.4	78	2	1808
Clam Chowder, New England, prepared with milk (1 cup)	248	6.6	3.0	163	22	992
Cream of Chicken, prepared with water (1 cup)	244	7.4	2.1	116	10	986
Cream of Mushroom, prepared with water (1 cup)	244	9.0	2.4	129	2	1031
Gazpacho, ready-to-serve (1 cup)	244	2.2	0.3	57	0	1183
Minestrone, chunky, ready-to-serve (1 cup)	240	2.8	1.5	127	5	864
Minestrone, prepared with water (1 cup)	241	2.5	0.5	83	2	911

FOOD DESCRIPTION/ PORTION	Wt. Gm	Tot. Fat Gm	Sat. Fat Gm	Cal.	Chol. Mg	Sod. Mg
Oyster Stew, prepared with milk (1 cup)	245	7.9	5.1	134	32	1040
Oyster Stew, prepared with water (1 cup)	241	3.8	2.5	59	14	980
Split Pea with Ham, prepared with water (1 cup)	253	4.4	1.8	189	8	1008
Tomato, prepared with water (1 cup)	244	1.9	0.4	86	0	872
Tomato Rice, prepared with water (1 cup)	247	2.7	0.5	120	2	815
Vegetarian Vegetable, prepared with water (1 cup)	241	1.9	0.3	72	0	823

Crackers

FOOD DESCRIPTION/ PORTION	Wt. Gm	Tot. Fat Gm	Sat. Fat Gm	Cal.	Chol. Mg	Sod. Mg
Bread Sticks, 7¾" x ¾" diameter (5)	25	0.8	0.2	96	0	175
Cheese Crackers (5)	16	13.4	1.3	75	—	163

FOOD DESCRIPTION/ PORTION	Wt. Gm	Tot. Fat Gm	Sat. Fat Gm	Cal.	Chol. Mg	Sod. Mg
Graham Crackers, 2½" squares (4)	28	2.6	0.6	110	—	190
Saltines (5 crackers)	14	1.7	0.4	62	—	156
Sandwich-Type, cheese-peanut butter (4 sandwiches)	28	6.8	1.8	139	—	281
Teething Crackers (2 pieces)	14	1.4	0.6	61	3	33
Baking Ingredients						
Cornmeal, dry (1 oz.)	28	0.3	—	100	—	0
Cornstarch, not packed (1 Tbsp.)	8	tr	0	29	—	0
Flour, white (1 oz.)	28	0.3	—	101	—	0

FOOD DESCRIPTION/ PORTION	Wt. Gm	Tot. Fat Gm	Sat. Fat Gm	Cal.	Chol. Mg	Sod. Mg

VEGETABLES AND FRUITS

Vegetables

FOOD DESCRIPTION/ PORTION	Wt. Gm	Tot. Fat Gm	Sat. Fat Gm	Cal.	Chol. Mg	Sod. Mg
All vegetables are low in fat and saturated fatty acids (½ to 1 cup)		0.2	0	25	0	*
Asparagus, frozen, cooked (4 spears)	60	0.3	0.1	17	0	2
Broccoli, cooked, boiled (¾ cup)	100	0.3	0	29	0	11
Garlic, raw (1 clove)	3	0	0	4	0	1
Kidney Beans, cooked, boiled (½ cup)	100	0.6	0.1	33	0	—
Lentils, cooked, stir-fried (½ cup)	100	0.5	0.1	101	0	—

* Sodium values vary from 2 to 63 milligrams per ½ cup cooked. Canned vegetables are higher in sodium than fresh or frozen.

FOOD DESCRIPTION/ PORTION	Wt. Gm	Tot. Fat Gm	Sat. Fat Gm	Cal.	Chol. Mg	Sod. Mg
Lima Beans, frozen, cooked (⅔ cup)	100	0.3	0.1	105	0	29
Mushrooms, raw (½ cup pieces)	35	0.2	0	9	0	1
Potato, baked, flesh and skin (1 potato)	202	0.2	0.1	220	0	16
Potato, boiled, cooked in skin, flesh (1 potato)	136	0.1	0	119	0	6
Squash, winter, all varieties, cooked (½ cup cubed)	100	0.6	0.1	39	0	1
Squash, zucchini, cooked, boiled (⅔ cup)	100	0.1	0	16	0	3
Tofu, raw, regular (¼ block)	116	5.6	0.8	88	0	8
Fruits						
Apple, raw, 2¾" diameter (1)	138	0.5	0.1	81	0	1

FOOD DESCRIPTION/ PORTION	Wt. Gm	Tot. Fat Gm	Sat. Fat Gm	Cal.	Chol. Mg	Sod. Mg
Applesauce, canned, unsweetened (½ cup)	140	0.1	0	61	0	2
Apricots, medium, raw (4)	141	0.6	0	68	0	1
Banana, 9" long (half)	57	0.3	0.1	53	0	1
Blackberries, raw (¾ cup)	108	0.4	0	56	0	0
Cantaloupe (1 cup cubes)	160	0.4	0	57	0	14
Cherries, sweet, raw (12)	82	0.8	0.2	59	0	0
Figs, raw (2 medium)	100	0.3	0	74	0	2
Fruit Cocktail, canned, juice-packed (½ cup)	136	0.1	0	62	0	4
Grapefruit (half)	123	0.1	0	37	0	0
Grapes, raw (15)	36	0.1	0	23	0	0
Honeydew Melon (1 cup cubes)	170	0.2	0	60	0	17
Kiwifruit (1 large)	91	0.4	0	55	0	4

FOOD DESCRIPTION/ PORTION	Wt. Gm	Tot. Fat Gm	Sat. Fat Gm	Cal.	Chol. Mg	Sod. Mg
Mango, raw (half)	104	0.3	0	68	0	2
Nectarine, 2½″ diameter (1)	136	0.6	0	67	0	0
Orange, 2½″ diameter (1)	131	0.2	0	62	0	0
Papaya (1 cup)	140	0.2	0.1	54	0	4
Peach, 2½″ diameter (1)	87	0.1	0	37	0	0
Peaches, canned, water-packed (2 halves)	154	0.1	0	36	0	6
Pear, raw (1)	166	0.7	0	98	0	1
Pineapple, raw (¾ cup)	116	0.5	0	58	0	2
Pineapple, canned, juice-packed (⅓ cup)	83	0.1	0	50	0	1
Plum, raw, 2⅛″ diameter (2)	132	0.8	0.1	72	0	0
Pomegranate (half)	77	0.2	0	52	0	3
Raspberries, raw (1 cup)	123	0.7	0	61	0	0
Strawberries, raw, whole (1¼ cups)	186	0.7	0	56	0	3

FOOD DESCRIPTION/ PORTION	Wt. Gm	Tot. Fat Gm	Sat. Fat Gm	Cal.	Chol. Mg	Sod. Mg
Tangerine, 2½" diameter (2)	168	0.3	0	74	0	2
Watermelon (2 cups cubes)	336	1.5	0	106	0	7

Dried Fruits

FOOD DESCRIPTION/ PORTION	Wt. Gm	Tot. Fat Gm	Sat. Fat Gm	Cal.	Chol. Mg	Sod. Mg
Apples, uncooked (6 rings)	42	0.2	0.2	100	0	36
Apricots, uncooked (12 halves)	42	0.2	0	97	0	3
Dates (5)	42	0.2	0	114	0	2
Figs, uncooked (2¼)	42	0.5	0.2	108	0	5
Prunes, uncooked (5)	42	0.2	0	101	0	2
Raisins (¼ cup)	42	0.2	0	124	0	4

Fruit Juices

FOOD DESCRIPTION/ PORTION	Wt. Gm	Tot. Fat Gm	Sat. Fat Gm	Cal.	Chol. Mg	Sod. Mg
Apple Juice (6 fluid oz.)	180	0.2	0	84	0	6
Cranberry Juice Cocktail (6 fluid oz.)	176	0	0	103	0	6

FOOD DESCRIPTION/ PORTION	Wt. Gm	Tot. Fat Gm	Sat. Fat Gm	Cal.	Chol. Mg	Sod. Mg
Grape Juice						
(6 fluid oz.)	180	0.2	0	111	0	4
Grapefruit Juice, unsweetened						
(6 fluid oz.)	180	0.2	0	68	0	3
Orange Juice						
(6 fluid oz.)	180	0.4	0	79	0	1
Pineapple Juice						
(6 fluid oz.)	180	0.1	0	101	0	1
Prune Juice						
(6 fluid oz.)	180	0	0	127	0	9

FOOD DESCRIPTION/ PORTION	Wt. Gm	Tot. Fat Gm	Sat. Fat Gm	Cal.	Chol. Mg	Sod. Mg
DESSERTS AND SNACKS						
Cakes, Cookies, Pies and Other Baked Goods						
Boston Cream Pie, 2-layer ($\frac{1}{12}$ of 8" diameter)	69	6.5	2.0	208	—	128
Brownies, with nuts and icing ($\frac{1}{6}$ of $7\frac{1}{2}$" x $5\frac{1}{4}$" x $\frac{7}{8}$" pan)	61	10.7	4.9	246	20	143
Cake, Angel Food, without frosting ($\frac{1}{12}$ of 10" diameter)	60	0.2	—	143	—	305
Cake, Devil's Food, without frosting, 2-layer ($\frac{1}{16}$ of 9" diameter)	56	8.7	3.4	179	—	319
Cake, Fruitcake, without frosting ($\frac{1}{32}$ of 7" diameter)	43	7.1	1.6	167	—	83

FOOD DESCRIPTION/ PORTION	Wt. Gm	Tot. Fat Gm	Sat. Fat Gm	Cal.	Chol. Mg	Sod. Mg
Cake, Pound Cake, without frosting (¹⁄₁₂ of 8½" loaf)	42	12.7	7.5	204	78	75
Cake, Sponge Cake, without frosting (¹⁄₁₂ of 9¾" diameter)	66	3.8	1.2	196	—	110
Cake, White, without frosting, 2-layer (¹⁄₁₆ of 9" diameter)	53	7.3	2.2	163	—	218
Cake, Yellow, 2-layer, without frosting (¹⁄₁₆ of 9" diameter)	54	8.4	1.9	181	—	234
Cake Frosting, chocolate, prepared with milk and fat (3 Tbsp.)	51	7.2	3.9	195	—	33
Cake Frosting, coconut, with boiled frosting (3 Tbsp.)	30	2.4	2.1	114	—	36

FOOD DESCRIPTION/ PORTION	Wt. Gm	Tot. Fat Gm	Sat. Fat Gm	Cal.	Chol. Mg	Sod. Mg
Cake Frosting, fudge, made with water (from mix) (3 Tbsp.)	45	3.0	0.9	156	—	108
Cake Frosting, white, boiled (3 Tbsp.)	18	0	0	57	—	24
Cheesecake (⅛ of 9" diameter)	100	19.2	—	302	—	222
Cookies, Chocolate Chip, 2⅓" diameter (3)	30	8.0	2.6	139	13	62
Cookies, Fig Bars (2)	28	1.9	0.5	106	—	90
Cookies, Gingersnaps, 2" diameter (4)	28	2.5	0.6	118	—	160
Cookies, sandwich, 1¾" diameter (3)	30	6.2	1.8	148	—	189
Cupcake, plain, no icing, 2½" diameter (2)	50	7.0	1.9	182	—	150

FOOD DESCRIPTION/ PORTION	Wt. Gm	Tot. Fat Gm	Sat. Fat Gm	Cal.	Chol. Mg	Sod. Mg
Cupcake, plain, with white uncooked icing, 2½" diameter (2)	70	8.2	2.7	256	—	158
Doughnut, cake-type, 3½" diameter (1)	25	5.8	1.2	105	8	139
Doughnut, yeast-type, 3¾" diameter (1)	42	11.2	2.7	172	8	99
Pastry, Danish, 4¼" diameter x 1" thick (1)	65	13.6	4.5	250	—	249
Pastry, toaster, commercial (1)	56	6.4	—	217	—	256
Pie, Apple, 2-crust (⅛ of 9" diameter)	118	11.9	3.4	282	—	181
Pie, Cherry, 2-crust (⅛ of 9" diameter)	118	13.3	3.5	308	—	359
Pie, Custard (⅛ of 9" diameter)	114	12.7	4.3	249	—	327
Pie, Pecan (⅛ of 9" diameter)	103	23.6	3.3	431	—	228

FOOD DESCRIPTION/ PORTION	Wt. Gm	Tot. Fat Gm	Sat. Fat Gm	Cal.	Chol. Mg	Sod. Mg
Pie, Pumpkin (⅛ of 9″ diameter)	114	12.8	4.5	241	—	244
Pie Crust, baked (⅛ of 9″ diameter)	23	7.5	1.8	113	—	138

Candy

FOOD DESCRIPTION/ PORTION	Wt. Gm	Tot. Fat Gm	Sat. Fat Gm	Cal.	Chol. Mg	Sod. Mg
Candy Corn (approx. 30 pieces)	42	0.9	0.2	155	—	90
Caramels, plain or chocolate (1½ oz.)	42	4.4	2.4	170	—	96
Chocolate- Coated Peanuts (1½ oz.)	42	17.6	4.5	239	—	26
Fudge, plain (1½ oz.)	42	5.3	1.8	170	—	81
Gumdrops (1½ oz.)	42	0.3	0	147	0	15
Hard Candy (1½ oz.)	42	0.5	0	164	0	14
Marshmallow (1½ oz.)	42	tr	0	135	0	17

FOOD DESCRIPTION/ PORTION	Wt. Gm	Tot. Fat Gm	Sat. Fat Gm	Cal.	Chol. Mg	Sod. Mg
Milk Chocolate, plain (1½ oz.)	42	13.8	7.7	221	—	41
Milk Chocolate, almond (1½ oz.)	42	15.2	6.8	227	—	35
Mints, uncoated (1½ oz.)	42	0.9	0.2	155	0	90

FOOD DESCRIPTION/ PORTION	Wt. Gm	Tot. Fat Gm	Sat. Fat Gm	Cal.	Chol. Mg	Sod. Mg
SAUCES AND GRAVIES						
Dehydrated Sauces						
Béarnaise, prepared with milk and butter (½ cup)	128	34.2	20.8	350	94	632
Cheese, prepared with milk (½ cup)	140	8.6	4.6	154	26	184
Hollandaise, prepared with milk and butter (½ cup)	128	34.2	21.0	352	94	568
Mushroom, prepared with water and vinegar (½ cup)	134	5.2	2.8	114	18	766
Sour Cream, prepared with milk (½ cup)	158	15.2	8.0	254	46	504
Stroganoff, prepared with milk and water (½ cup)	148	5.4	3.4	136	20	914

FOOD DESCRIPTION/ PORTION	Wt. Gm	Tot. Fat Gm	Sat. Fat Gm	Cal.	Chol. Mg	Sod. Mg
Sweet and Sour, prepared with water and vinegar (½ cup)	156	0	0	148	0	390
White, prepared with milk (½ cup)	132	6.8	3.2	120	18	398
Ready-to-Serve Sauces						
Barbecue (½ Tbsp.)	16	0.3	0	12	0	127
Soy (1 Tbsp.)	18	0	0	11	0	1029
Teriyaki (1 Tbsp.)	18	0	0	15	0	690
Canned Gravies						
Au jus (½ cup)	120	0.2	0.2	20	0	—
Beef (½ cup)	116	2.7	1.4	62	4	59
Chicken (½ cup)	119	6.8	1.7	95	3	688
Mushroom (½ cup)	120	3.2	0.4	60	0	680
Turkey (½ cup)	120	2.6	0.8	62	2	—
Dehydrated Gravies						
Au jus, prepared with water (½ cup)	124	0.4	0.2	10	0	290

FOOD DESCRIPTION/ PORTION	Wt. Gm	Tot. Fat Gm	Sat. Fat Gm	Cal.	Chol. Mg	Sod. Mg
Brown, prepared with water (½ cup)	130	0.2	0	44	tr	62
Chicken, prepared with water (½ cup)	130	1.0	0.2	42	2	566
Mushroom, prepared with water (½ cup)	128	0.4	0.2	36	0	702
Onion, prepared with water (½ cup)	130	0.4	0.2	40	0	518
Pork, prepared with water (½ cup)	128	1.0	0.4	38	2	618
Turkey, prepared with water (½ cup)	130	1.0	0.3	44	2	750

USDA HANDBOOK NO. 8 SERIES

Series No.	Food Group Issued	Year
8–1	Dairy and Egg Products	1976
8–2	Spices and Herbs	1977
8–3	Baby Foods	1978
8–4	Fats and Oils	1979
8–5	Poultry Products	1979
8–6	Soups, Sauces and Gravies	1980
8–7	Sausages and Luncheon Meats	1980
8–8	Breakfast Cereals	1982
8–9	Fruits and Fruit Juices	1982
8–10	Pork Products	1983
8–11	Vegeables and Vegetable Products	1984
8–12	Nut and Seed Products	1984
8–13	Beef Products	1990
8–14	Beverages	1986
8–15	Finfish and Shellfish Products	1987
8–16	Legumes and Legume Products	1986
8–17	Lamb, Veal and Game Products	1989
8–20	Cereal, Grains and Pasta	1989
8–21	Fast Foods	1988

USDA Handbook No. 456, 1975.

USDA Provisional Table on the Fatty Acids and Cholesterol Content of Selected Foods, 1984.

USDA Provisional Table on the Nutrient Content of Bakery Foods and Related Items.